SCIENCE BUZZWORDS

Is It Shiny?

For a free color catalog describing Gareth Stevens Publishing's list of high-quality books and multimedia programs, call 1-800-542-2595 (USA) or 1-800-461-9120 (Canada). Gareth Stevens Publishing's Fax: (414) 225-0377.
See our catalog, too, on the World Wide Web: http://gsinc.com

Library of Congress Cataloging-in-Publication Data

Bryant-Mole, Karen.
    Is it shiny? / Karen Bryant-Mole.
       p. cm. — (Science buzzwords)
    Includes index.
    Summary: Text and pictures introduce a variety of antonyms such as transparent and opaque, shiny and dull, and hard and soft.
    ISBN 0-8368-1728-1 (lib. bdg.)
     1. Vocabulary—Juvenile literature. 2. Science—Juvenile literature.
[1. English language—Synonyms and antonyms. 2. Vocabulary.]
I. Title. II. Series.
PE1449.B794   1997
428.1—dc20   96-38740

First published in North America in 1997 by
Gareth Stevens Publishing
1555 North RiverCenter Drive, Suite 201
Milwaukee, WI 53212 USA

This edition © 1997 by Gareth Stevens, Inc. Original edition published in 1995 by A & C Black (Publishers) Limited, 35 Bedford Row, London, England, WC1R 4JH. Text © 1995 by Karen Bryant-Mole. Photographs © 1995 by Zul Mukhida, except page 17 Eye Ubiquitous. Additional end matter © 1997 by Gareth Stevens, Inc.

The author and publisher would like to thank all the children who appear in the photographs.

Printed in the United States of America

1 2 3 4 5 6 7 8 9 01 00 99 98 97

SCIENCE BUZZWORDS

Is It Shiny?

Karen Bryant-Mole

Gareth Stevens Publishing
MILWAUKEE

liquid

Yasmin is pouring some milk.
Anything that can be poured is a **liquid**.

solid

Now she is eating a piece of cake.
Cake cannot be poured. It is a **solid**.

hard

Tim knocks on a door.
The door feels **hard**.

soft

He goes inside and takes off his shoes.
The rug he sits on feels **soft**.

stretchy

Lou has **stretchy** suspenders.
When he pulls on them, they get longer.

springy

This **springy** foam ball will always
go back to its round shape.

wet

Sarah has been swimming.
Her swimsuit is **wet**.

dry

Sarah is done swimming for the day.
She has changed into **dry** clothes.

rough

This pineapple feels **rough**.
Its skin is bumpy.

smooth

A mango has **smooth** skin.
It feels flat and even.

firm

This spaghetti hasn't been cooked yet.
It is **firm**, or hard.

flexible

Cooked spaghetti is soft and **flexible**.
Thomas can wind it around his fork.

shiny

Yasmin is wearing a pretty coat.
It is a bright, **shiny** raincoat.

dark

Lou's raincoat is not shiny.
It is **dark** and absorbs the light.

furry

Sarah likes to pet her cat, Samantha.
Samantha's coat feels soft and **furry**.

prickly

This porcupine has **prickly** spines.
The spines feel sharp.

patterned

Lou's shorts are **patterned**.
There are lots of different shapes on them.

plain

Vusa's sweater is all one color.
There are no shapes on it. It is **plain**.

gritty

Sand is made from tiny pieces of rock.
It feels rough and **gritty**.

powdery

Powdery things, like after-bath powders, feel soft and smooth.

transparent

You can see through Vusa's glass.
The glass is **transparent**, or clear.

opaque

You can't see through Yasmin's
drinking cup. It is **opaque**.

How to Use This Book

Children's understanding of concepts is fundamentally linked to their ability to comprehend and use relevant language. This book is designed to help children understand the vocabulary associated with **materials**.

Materials are an important part of science. They are the foundation upon which chemistry is built. Some materials, such as plastic and glass, are manufactured by humans. Other materials, such as sand and water, can be found in nature.

Grouping materials and describing their properties are essential scientific skills. This book helps children develop those skills by explaining key words connected to the properties of materials and by encouraging children to look for similarities and differences between materials.

Each word in this book is presented through a color photograph and a phrase, which uses the word in context. Some of the pairs of words featured on each double page, such as *hard* and *soft*, are opposites. Other pairs of words, such as *furry* and *prickly*, are not opposites. Children can be encouraged to discuss which pairs are opposites and which are not.

Besides explaining words basic to the understanding of materials, the book can also be used in a number of other ways.

Children can think of, or find, objects other than the one in the photographs that can be described using a particular Science Buzzword. The Buzzword, *opaque*, for example does not just describe cups. It can be applied to a variety of objects. Teddy bears, tree trunks, pencils, apples, and sweaters are all *opaque*.

The book can be used to help a child further define the properties of a particular object. For instance, materials can often be described using more than one word. A stone might be described as being *hard*, *smooth*, and *opaque*.

Children can be encouraged to think about the uses of the different properties and how this makes an object suitable for particular functions. Why is *stretchy* elastic best for suspenders? Why is *hard* wood good for doors? How do a porcupine's *prickly* spines protect the animal from harm?

The properties of materials aren't always constant. Water is a *liquid* that can be frozen into a *solid*. Clay is *soft* but when it is baked, it becomes *hard*. Clothes in a washing machine are *wet*. But when they are hung for a time on a clothesline, they become *dry*. Children can think about whether the properties of any other materials always stay the same. If not, how and why do they change?

For Further Study —
Activities

1. **Collections** — Make collections of different types of objects, such as objects that are *shiny* or *smooth*. Then decorate some old shoe boxes, and use them to store your collections. Glue one of the objects on top of each lid as a reminder of what's inside.

2. **Ice Cubes: Liquid or Solid?** — Ask an adult to help you make some fruit juice ice cubes. When you pour the juice into the ice cube tray, it is a *liquid*. Once the juice has frozen, it can no longer be poured, and it is a *solid*. What happens if you put the frozen cubes into a cup and leave them for a while?

3. **Toy Models** — There are various household materials that can be used to make toy models. Egg cartons could become a crocodile's *rough* skin. Foil would make a robot look *shiny*. A cotton ball is perfect for a rabbit's *soft* tail. What other materials do you see in the house?

4. **What Am I Thinking?** — Play this guessing game with your friends. Describe an object using only the Science Buzzwords in this book. For example, say, "I'm thinking of something *smooth* and *transparent*." Can your friends guess that you are thinking of a window?

5. **Mystery Boxes** — With an adult's help, cut a large hole in the end of a shoebox, just big enough for someone's hand to fit inside. Then put an item, such as a small toy or a stone in the box. Put the cover on the box. Have a friend guess what's inside your mystery box by feeling the object.

6. **Science Experiment** — Take two ice cubes that are the same size out of the freezer, and place each one in a small bowl. Put one bowl outside, and leave the other one in the kitchen. Which cube melts and turns from a *solid* to a *liquid* first? Repeat your experiment by placing cubes in other places, like one in the sun and the other in the shade. Do the results of the experiment change depending on the season?

7. **Wrapping Paper** — Decorate brown paper, such as a large paper bag, with paint to make colorful wrapping paper. Use a rubber stamp, old cookie cutter, or piece of sponge to apply the paint in a pattern. Use your patterned paper to wrap a special present.

8. **Nature Hunt** — Go on a Buzzword "treasure hunt" in your backyard or a neighborhood park. Can you find something in nature to fit each of the Science Buzzwords in this book? What can you find that is *prickly*? What is *rough*?

9. **Clay Art** — With an adult's help, roll out a large piece of clay with a rolling pin or glass. Then make a pattern in the clay by pressing in small objects, such as a pencil eraser or paper clip. Your pattern should repeat itself, such as five circles made by the eraser, followed by two paper clip shapes, followed by five more circles and two paper clip shapes.

Places to Visit

Betty Brinn Children's Museum
929 East Wisconsin Avenue
Milwaukee, WI 53202

Children's Museum
Museum Wharf
300 Congress Street
Boston, MA 02210

Children's Museum of Indianapolis
3000 North Meridian Street
Indianapolis, IN 46206

Discovery Place
301 North Tryon Street
Charlotte, NC 28202

Discovery World
712 West Wells Street
Milwaukee, WI 53233

Exploratorium
3601 Lyon Street
San Francisco, CA 94123

Los Angeles Children's Museum
310 North Main Street
Los Angeles, CA 90012

Museum of Science and Industry
57th Street and Lake Shore Drive
Chicago, IL 60637

Ontario Science Center
770 Don Mills Road
North York, Ontario M3C 1T3

Science Center of British Columbia
1455 Quebec Street
Vancouver, British Columbia V6A 3Z7

Science Museum Of Minnesota
30 East Tenth Street
St. Paul, MN 55101

The Smithsonian Institution
Information Center
1000 Jefferson Drive SW
Washington, D.C. 20560

Books

Explorabook: A Kids' Science Museum in a Book. Jim Cassidy (Klutz Press)

Exploring Our Senses (series). Henry Pluckrose (Gareth Stevens)

First Step Science (series). Kay Davies and Wendy Oldfield (Gareth Stevens)

Hands-On Science (series). (Gareth Stevens)

How to Be a Nature Detective. Millicent Selsam (HarperCollins)

The Magic School Bus: Science Explorations. (Scholastic)

My First Science Book. Angela Wilkes (Knopf)

Science Arts. Mary Ann Kohl and Jean Potter (Bright Ring Publishing)

The Science Book of Water. Neil Ardley (Harcourt, Brace, Jovanovich)

Silly Science. Shar Levine and Leslie Johnstone (John Wiley & Sons)

Solid, Liquid, or Gas? Fay Robinson (Childrens Press)

Web Sites

http://www.waterw.com/~science/kids.html

http://www.islandnet.com/~yesmag/

Videos

I Like Science. (Concord Video)

Me and My Senses. (Phoenix/BFA Films and Video)

Minnie's Science Field Trips. (Coronet, The Multimedia Group)

My First Science Video. (Sony)

Science Rock. (Kimbo Educational)

Seeing Things. (Beacon Films)

Skin Deep. (Films for the Humanities and Sciences)

Index